·····▶ REICH

FOR BEGINNERS

DAVID ZANE MAIROWITZ

ILLUSTRATED BY GERMAN GONZALES

GLOBE

JEWISH PORNOGRAPHER

OSLO POST

God Reich creates LIFE

YOU CAN'T HAVE A POLITICAL AND ECONOMIC REVOLUTION WITHOUT A SEXUAL REVOLUTION

...THIS IS BEGINNING TO SOUND LESS AND LESS LIKE PSYCHOANALYSIS AND MORE AND MORE LIKE —GASP— POLITICS!!!

Writers and Readers

WRITERS & READERS ...CKS London · Sydney

10683698

This edition first published by
Writers and Readers Publishing Cooperative
in association with
Unwin Paperbacks 1986

A *Writers and Readers* ◄▬ Documentary Comic Book © 1986

UNWIN ® PAPERBACKS
40 Museum Street, London WC1A 1LU, UK

Unwin Paperbacks
Park Lane, Hemel Hempstead, Herts HP2 4TE, UK

Writers and Readers Publishing Cooperative Society Limited
144 Camden High Street, London NW1 0NE, UK

Writers and Readers Publishing Inc.
500 Fifth Avenue, New York NY 10110

George Allen & Unwin Australia Pty Ltd
8 Napier Street, North Sydney, NSW 2060, Australia

Unwin Paperbacks with the Port Nicholson Press
PO Box 11–838, Wellington, New Zealand

ISBN 0 04 921032 7

Printed in Great Britain by
Richard Clay (The Chaucer Press) Ltd,
Bungay, Suffolk

·····▶ REICH

FOR BEGINNERS

CAN WE CLEAR THE AIR IN PEOPLE TOO?

IN A WAY, JA...

PEOPLE KEEP BACK THEIR EMOTIONS
THEY DON'T LET THE ENERGY STREAM,
THEY ARE AFRAID OF FEELING GOOD. AND
THEY TRY TO STOP THEIR CHILDREN FROM
FEELING GOOD TOO. THEY
BLOCK THEIR NATURAL INSTINCTS — JUST
LIKE THE AIR IN THE SKY IS NOW
BLOCKED — AND INSTEAD OF
COMING OUT FREELY, THE ENERGY
GETS LOCKED UP.
THEIR STOMACHS GET TIGHT,
BREATH COMES SHORT,
THEIR LIPS GO RIGID AND
THEY LIVE BEHIND A MASK.
SOON
THEY BEGIN TO HATE.
BECAUSE THEY ARE AFRAID TO BE HAPPY.
AFRAID TO BE FREE.

4

to be continued . . .

Wilhelm Reich's life-long battle with the Death Instinct begins on 24th March, 1897 (really it begins some forty weeks earlier) in Dobrzcynica, in that part of Galicia belonging to the Austrian Empire. Later in life he will always be secretive about his personal life, not so much is known about his early days.

7

There is someone else in Vienna who thinks along the same lines.

1920

Reich pays his first visit to Dr Sigmund Freud, and the same year joins the Vienna Psychoanalytic Society.

8

1922 He becomes a clinical assistant in Freud's Psychoanalytic Polyclinic.

Reich is strongly interested in Freud's theories, especially:

1. Human life is, to a great extent, controlled by the UNCONSCIOUS in dreams, slips of the tongue, etc.

2. Sex and procreation are not the same thing. The evidence is to be found in the already alert sexuality of small children. If this infant sexuality is repressed it will later turn into adult NEUROSIS.

But Reich will be, all his life, chiefly influenced by Freud's idea of

3. LIBIDO: drive energy in human beings which is primarily sexual, although Freud believed there were other important instincts at work and that NOT EVERYTHING is connected to SEX. Not so for WR...

9

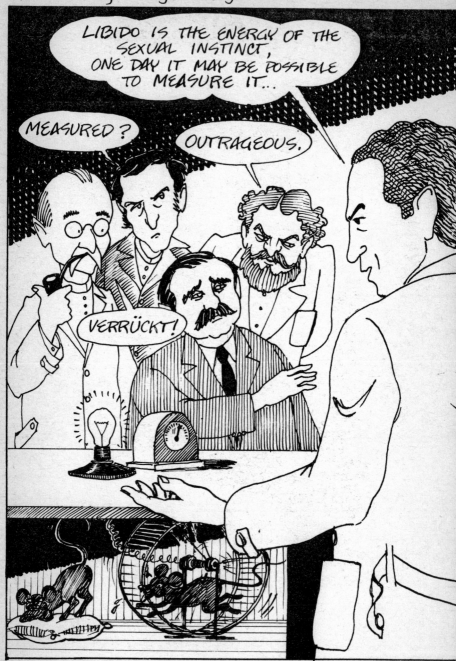

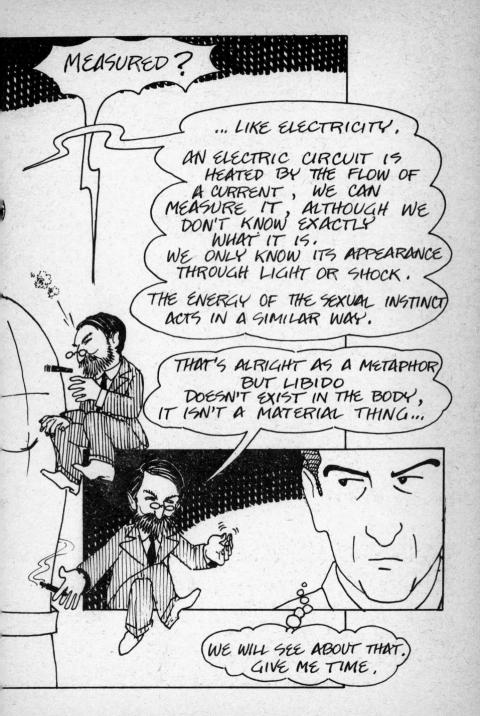

11

In 1927 he asked Freud to give him personal psychoanalysis but Freud refused. Too bad.

If only he'd gone through with it, he might have heard some strong truths delivered on his famous couch

...I ADORED MY MOTHER...

13

Reich's questioning of Freud's methods will always brand him as a heretic in the psychoanalytic circles of Vienna.

Sooner or later these two doctors are going to fall out irreversibly, in large part because Reich will insist on the SEXUAL BASIS for every neurosis.

❋ hobby-horse.

But something else is troubling WR at the time...

Up to this point Psychoanalysis recognises only erective and ejaculative potency in male patients. It sets out to achieve these as a basis for sexual health. But for Reich this is not enough. Erection and even ejaculation are only pre-requisites for what he calls 'orgastic potency'. And in 1923 he develops his revolutionary...

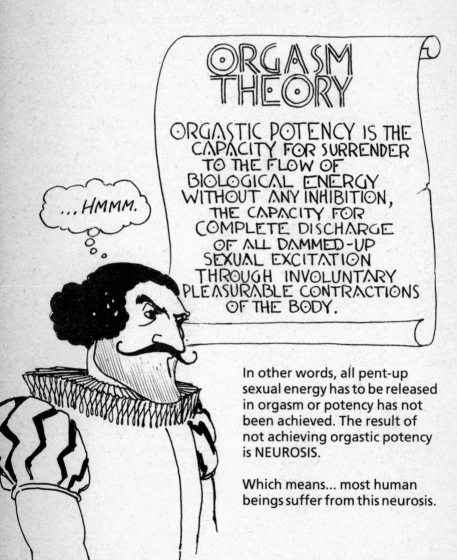

ORGASM THEORY

ORGASTIC POTENCY IS THE CAPACITY FOR SURRENDER TO THE FLOW OF BIOLOGICAL ENERGY WITHOUT ANY INHIBITION, THE CAPACITY FOR COMPLETE DISCHARGE OF ALL DAMMED-UP SEXUAL EXCITATION THROUGH INVOLUNTARY PLEASURABLE CONTRACTIONS OF THE BODY.

...HMMM.

In other words, all pent-up sexual energy has to be released in orgasm or potency has not been achieved. The result of not achieving orgastic potency is NEUROSIS.

Which means... most human beings suffer from this neurosis.

16

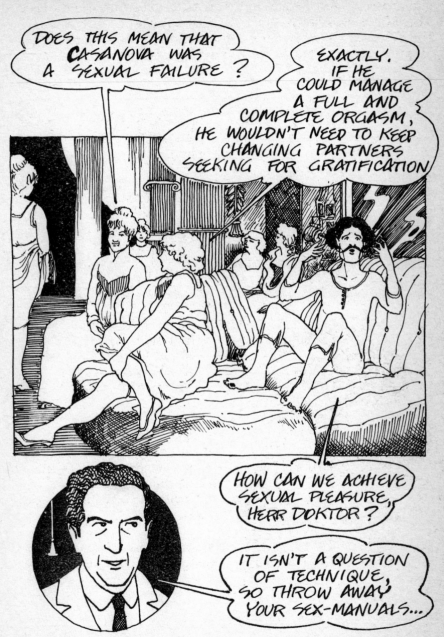

-OK!...WE CAN START WITH FOREPLAY, BUT DON'T GET LOST IN IT...

SOONER OR LATER PLEASURE HAS TO BE CONCENTRATED IN THE GENITALS. FREUD AND HIS FOLLOWERS ALWAYS TALK OF 'SEXUAL SATISFACTION', BUT IT'S REALLY 'GENITAL SATISFACTION' THAT'S THE KEY TO HEALTH.

WHAT NOW, DOKTOR?

-PATIENCE!
YOU ACHIEVE PENETRATION AND ALL YOUR MOVEMENTS MUST BE SLOW AND GENTLE...

IF YOU HURRY, YOU'RE LIVING OUT SOME SADISTIC URGE AGAINST YOUR PARTNER. AND YOU MUST BE EQUAL, BOTH OF YOU...

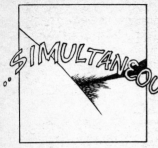  

...SIMULTANEOUS RHYTHMIC MOVEMENTS...

...THERE MUST BE HARMONY BETWEEN YOU.

THIS SOUNDS LIKE A SEX MANUAL

...RUHE! NO TALKING! NO DISTRACTIONS PLEASE, IT KEEPS YOUR MIND TOO ACTIVE. SO FAR EVERYTHING HAS BEEN TOO CONSCIOUS, TOO CONTROLLED. YOU MUST KEEP YOUR RHYTHM...

...AND LET IT ALL BECOME INVOLUNTARY

LOSE YOURSELVES IN IT...

 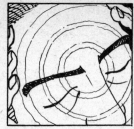 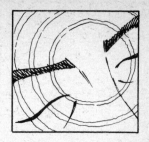

THE PELVIS NOW SWINGS EASILY, WITHOUT EFFORT,
EXCITEMENT SPREADS THROUGHOUT THE BODY
AS THE MUSCLES CONTRACT...

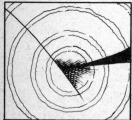 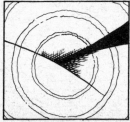 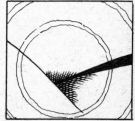

YOU BREATHE DEEP, YOUR HEART BEATS FASTER...

 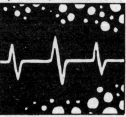 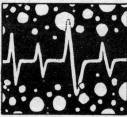

THE BODY SWEATS AND BEGINS TO CONVULSE,
JUST BEFORE ORGASM, CONSCIOUSNESS IS ECLIPSED,

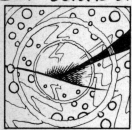  

ENERGY IS CONCENTRATED IN THE GENITALS
AND, WHEN DISCHARGED, IT FLOWS THROUGH
THE WHOLE BODY...

20

THIS COMPLETE FLOWING BACK OF THE EXCITATION TOWARDS THE WHOLE BODY IS WHAT CONSTITUTES GRATIFICATION.

IT'S TRUE... I DON'T FEEL EXHAUSTED AND LET DOWN AS I USUALLY DO.

THAT WAS GREAT...

NOT FOR ME

...REICH OBSERVES THAT HIS PATIENTS REMAIN LUCID AND CONSCIOUS DURING SEX. THIS MEANS THAT NOT ALL THE SEXUAL ENERGY HAS BEEN RELEASED DURING ORGASM. SOME REMAINS TRAPPED.

HE CALLS THIS 'SEXUAL STASIS'. THIS UNSPENT ENERGY FEEDS THE NEUROTIC SYMPTOM OF THE PATIENT.

It seems then that orgastic IMPOTENCY is not an effect of neurosis – as most psychoanalysts think – but its CAUSE. That is to say, people become ill because they can't achieve satisfactory orgasm. Only a proper and full release of sexual energy can lead to mental health.

WELL THEN, IT SEEMS YOU CAN DO WITHOUT ME...

NOT REALLY... I'LL COME BACK TO YOU IN A MINUTE...

SOMETHING SEEMS TO **INTERFERE** WITH THE PROPER RELEASE OF SEXUAL ENERGY. I MUST FIND OUT WHAT'S GETTING IN THE WAY...

Reich realises that what Freud saw as the cause of neuroses was really the CONTENT, the material for fantasy supplied to the neuroses. The infantile fantasies discovered by Freud, such as the Oedipus Complex, are carried into the sex act and prohibit free love making. Men who fantasise rape or violence during sex have sadistic tendencies going back to childhood.

These infantile fixations have to be eliminated – presumably
through psychoanalysis – before genital health can be restored.

IN FACT, ALL IRRELEVANT FANTASIES MUST GO.

Proper orgasm must be
free, involuntary,
(you mustn't be trying
to have one),
specifically genital,
of a certain
duration
and...
decidedly
HETEROSEXUAL.

NO
PERVERSIONS
PLEASE.

23

CRITIQUE #1
W.R. IS GENITALLY OBSESSIVE

Reich is expecting an orgasm which most people will never achieve. Moreover, he fails to distinguish between male and female sexuality, a distinction which often shows that sexual pleasure need not be based totally on the idea of genital surrender. Clitoral stimulation is also a function of sexual satisfaction in women, for instance, and does not even require a male partner. Also, his life-long views on male homosexuality are, in a word, Neanderthal, especially for a man of his sensitivity. Like most analysts of his day, he considers it an aberration that requires curing. Although he himself won't have anything to do with such 'cure'. It is reported that he never took on a homosexual patient and, when once asked to do so, responded:

'Ich will mit solchen Schweinereien nichts zu tun haben' (I won't have anything to do with such filth...) ■

What are the implications of the ORGASM THEORY?
They are truly revolutionary

The orgasm is no longer a mere biological function used in procreation, nor the side effect of casual pleasure...

IT IS THE VERY CENTRE OF HUMAN EXPERIENCE AND ULTIMATELY DETERMINES THE HAPPINESS OF THE HUMAN RACE

Reich writes all this down in his book *DIE FUNKTION DES ORGASMUS* and on May 6, 1926, dedicates a copy to Freud...

This is not Reich's first run-in with the Old Man, nor will it be the last. In fact, he is about to challenge the Master's theory and practice more than ever with his own great contribution to psychoanalytic theory: CHARACTER ANALYSIS.

CHARACTER ANALYSIS

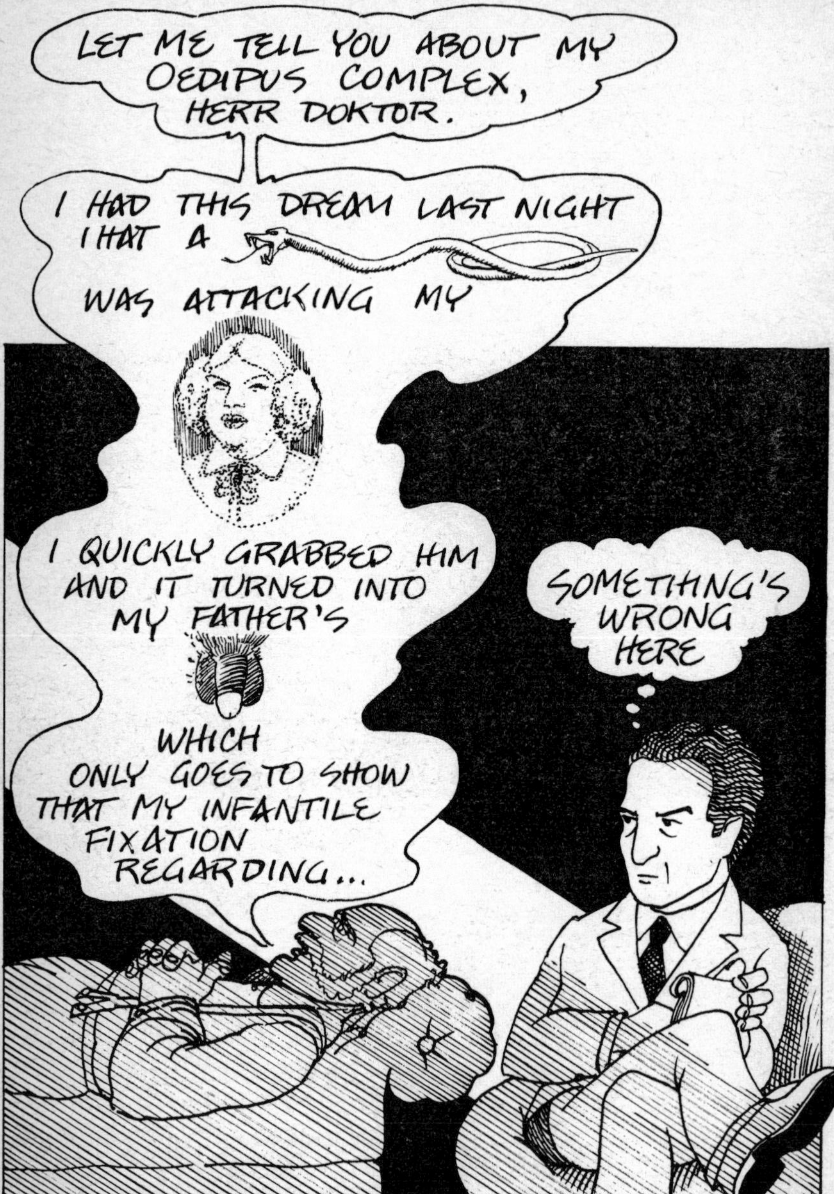

Reich notices that many patients are 'resisting' analysis. Some simply object to revealing personal secrets; others, however, are only too happy to do so. They are over-polite and helpful.

Reich compares the unconscious to geological layers of the earth. Each layer is formed during a different 'era' in someone's personal history. Psychoanalysts should proceed like geologists, first cutting through the surface to get at the depths.

Freud and his followers tend, generally speaking, to go for the deeper meaning without first examining the surface.

But despite the Old Man's resistance to his analysis, WR never looks back.

If a neurotic symptom comes from a specific problem or desire in the patient's past (as Freud concluded) then the Character Neurosis is the result of his entire life-history.

Reich has come to believe that

CHARACTER ITSELF IS A DISEASE.

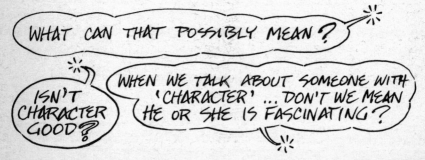

WHAT CAN THAT POSSIBLY MEAN?

ISN'T CHARACTER GOOD?

WHEN WE TALK ABOUT SOMEONE WITH 'CHARACTER'... DON'T WE MEAN HE OR SHE IS FASCINATING?

During analysis, Reich watches how his patients walk, stand, sit, carry themselves, listens to their tone of voice even more than what they say...

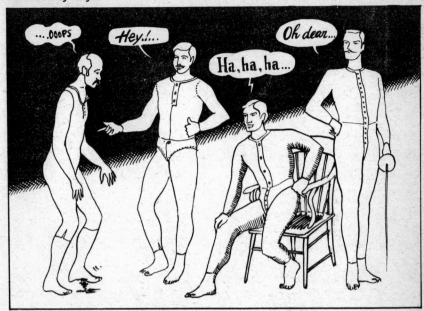

He concludes that people form a kind of ARMOUR to protect themselves, not only from the blows of the outside world, but also from their own desires and instincts. Most of us desire something and immediately set out to find ways NOT to get it! Reich sees this process working in the body. Over the years a person builds up his

CHARACTER ARMOUR

through bodily habits and typical attitudes of physical behaviour.

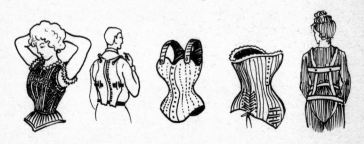

Just about this time Reich treats a patient
who nearly always smiles in an ironic way:

Reich tries to show the character trait to the patient so he can analyse its meaning. He confronts him with it over and over again until the patient begins to feel it as an illness he wants to get rid of.

SO WHO'S GOT CHARACTER ARMOUR THEN?

Just about everyone to some degree, although some people are more armoured than others.

During the period of Character Analysis Reich realises something else.

He begins to take a more active role in the analysis, intervening, contradicting the patient and even involving himself emotionally...

Character Analysis also gives rise sometimes to violent outbursts...

But even with Freud's opposition, Character Analysis becomes the only part of Reich's work to be accepted by the psychoanalytic movement. The Orgasm Theory is dismissed, even though for Reich Orgastic Potency is the GOAL of Character Analysis. Reich asks himself where the unspent energy of an unsatisfactory orgasm goes...

IT TURNS INTO **CHARACTER.** THE ROLE OF ORGASM (A SATISFACTORY ONE) IS TO LIBERATE THIS ENERGY FROM THE PRISON OF CHARACTER

BUT...

.. HANG ON A MINUTE HERR DOKTOR. SURELY OUR CHARACTER IS FORMING LONG BEFORE WE EVEN KNOW WHAT AN ORGASM IS

...JA, RICHTIG

Reich realises that character armour is not a NATURAL human development. If left completely to their positive instincts most people would turn into

GENITAL CHARACTERS,

capable of full and free orgastic potency.

But something goes wrong right from the start...

JUST WHAT KIND OF LIFE IS THIS ANYWAY?

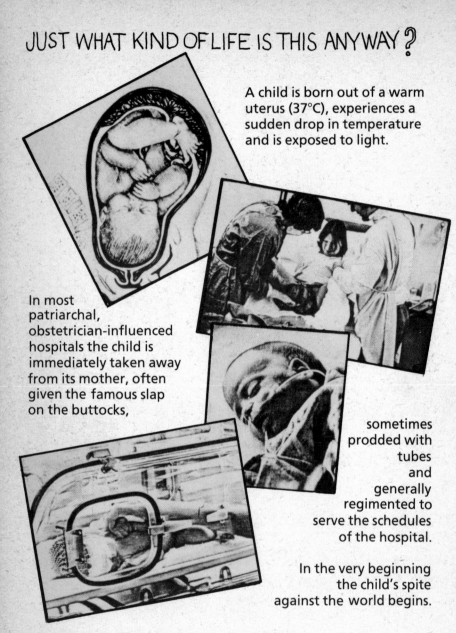

A child is born out of a warm uterus (37°C), experiences a sudden drop in temperature and is exposed to light.

In most patriarchal, obstetrician-influenced hospitals the child is immediately taken away from its mother, often given the famous slap on the buttocks,

sometimes prodded with tubes and generally regimented to serve the schedules of the hospital.

In the very beginning the child's spite against the world begins.

Later, when Reich becomes politically committed, he will wonder how many times a child is hated before it's even born.

But the torture is only just beginning. The road blocks to orgastic potency are being set up right away by that social institution which Reich is about to make his life-long enemy: **the**

FAMILY

Reich identifies THREE PHASES in which the Family turns its children into armoured characters.

Infancy

Sexual inhibition in children leads to psychic inhibition, to a lack of independent thought and action. The child then forms a complete fixation and dependence on the parents. Most neuroses develop in...

THE BASIS OF THE PUBERTY PROBLEM IS SOCIOLOGICAL, NOT BIOLOGICAL

THE ADOLESCENT IS MADE SUBMISSIVE SO HE OR SHE WILL BE READY FOR **COMPULSIVE MARRIAGE**

!

REMEMBER, **ONE** PARTNER FOR LIFE

By the age of 13, in some cases even earlier, a young person is ready to make love. The earlier he or she does so, the less likely he or she is to agree to the one-partner-for-life swindle.

AFTER ALL,

YOU WOULDN'T WEAR THE SAME CLOTHES ALL YEAR ROUND, WOULD YOU?

42

When the sexual happiness of youth has been stifled, creating inevitable neuroses, these problems are carried into...

PHASE 3

Marriage

Premarital continence, instead of preparing the way for happy marriage, often leads to further sexual difficulties. Sexual needs can only be gratified by one partner for a limited time. Compulsive monogamy then feeds the continuing neuroses, leading to a breakdown in Marriage. Why does it have to be like this?

COMPULSIVE MARRIAGE AND THE COMPULSIVE FAMILY GO ON RECREATING THE HUMAN STRUCTURE OF THIS ECONOMICALLY AND PSYCHICALLY MECHANISED AGE

...THIS IS BEGINNING TO SOUND LESS AND LESS LIKE PSYCHOANALYSIS AND MORE AND MORE LIKE —GASP—

POLITICS!!!

Reich's politics will always cause trouble among the psychoanalytic crowd. Just after the First World War two progressive movements like Marxism and psychoanalysis were not so incompatible as they later became. Reich finds himself attracted to both and will seek to bring them together.

During the 1920's, as Reich's political commitment grows, the psychoanalytical movement becomes respectable and conservative. Reich sees that it serves only the rich and privileged, and wonders about everybody else...

THEN IN VIENNA, IN 1927, at a workers' demonstration...

That very day, Reich joins the Austrian Communist Party. He had already been a member of the Socialist Party but now sees it selling out to the bourgeoisie. He begins reading Marx and Engels and finds himself under their influence.

He examines the 'sexual misery of the masses' and discovers there is no contraceptive information available, illegal unhygienic abortions are commonplace, children suffer from compulsive marriage between ill-matched parents. Also – a theme he will come back to many times – adolescents who want to make love have nowhere to go.

In 1928, Reich and his colleagues found the Socialist Society for Sex Consultation and Sexological Research (Sozialistische Gesellschaft für Sexualberatung und Sexualforschung). The following year they establish the first sex-hygiene centres for workers and employees (Sexualberatungsklinik für Arbeiter und Angestellte) in Vienna.

But most of the problems brought to Reich still concern the FAMILY as such. In the Communist classics he finds some inspiration.

THE BOURGEOIS FAMILY WILL VANISH AS A MATTER OF COURSE WITH THE VANISHING OF CAPITAL

BUT IT IS ENGELS WHO REALLY TURNS THE KEY

"What will be new after the overthrow of capitalist production? A new generation of men who never in their lives have known what it is to buy a woman's surrender with money or any other instrument of social power; a generation of women who have never known what it is to give themselves to a man from any other consideration than real love or to refuse to give themselves to their lover from fear of the economic consequences."

ORIGIN OF THE FAMILY BY FRIEDRICH ENGELS

YOU CAN'T HAVE A SEXUAL REVOLUTION WITHOUT A POLITICAL AND ECONOMIC REVOLUTION

He also finds a social explanation for the phenomenon of compulsive monogamy, reading, as Engels did, the work of Lewis Morgan, a Victorian anthropologist. Morgan believes primitive societies were based on the principle of communal marriage. Only with the growth of private property does the patriarchal family come into being, with Papa as central authority-figure.

Reich begins to see, in the typical family structure, a model for the whole of authoritarian society...

This is all leading to a final showdown with his own father figure, Dr Freud.

For one thing, Reich's new critique throws out the idea of psychoanalytic 'neutrality'. The analyst should take sides against society's enforcement of sexual repression.

More important: he should work to PREVENT neuroses on a MASS SCALE rather than simply cure individual ones. In short, become POLITICAL.

At this point, they would have done well to exchange names:
Freud = Joy; Reich = Empire.

What is this new argument about?

It is a matter of LIFE and DEATH.

In 1929, Freud writes CIVILISATION AND ITS
DISCONTENTS, arguing that society NEEDS
the suppression of instincts if it is to
flourish and survive.

Excess sexual energy should be diverted
towards more lofty goals in the service
of society.

THE LIBERTY OF THE INDIVIDUAL IS NOT A BENEFIT TO CULTURE...

THE OLD MAN IS BECOMING A REACTIONARY

PEOPLE WORK BETTER IF THEY SUBLIMATE THEIR SEXUAL INSTINCTS

WRONG AGAIN, HERR DOKTOR, IF THEY CHECK THEIR INSTINCTS THEY BECOME SICK.

IF THEY ARE NEUROTIC THEY WILL BE UNABLE TO ADJUST CULTURALLY.

Freud had earlier developed the idea that the energy drive of basic unconscious desires and instincts was a more or less free agent he called the PLEASURE PRINCIPLE. Now he begins to get worried about it...

PEOPLE NEED A **REALITY PRINCIPLE** TO KEEP THE PLEASURE PRINCIPLE UNDER CONTROL. OTHERWISE WE'D HAVE **ANARCHY**

THE RULING CLASS HAS A REALITY PRINCIPLE WHICH SERVES THE PERPETUATION OF ITS POWER!

So the Old Man is RIGHT... Society DOES NEED the repression of natural impulses. But not in order to grow into a healthy society, as Freud believes. Just the opposite: this makes people docile and blindly responsive to authority.

What makes Freud take this negative view? He has seen the human horror of the Big War and thinks that sadism and violence are natural instincts. In THE FUTURE OF AN ILLUSION he goes so far as to say that DEATH is the ultimate aim of LIFE; moreover...

Now the Old Man is really slipping away into dangerous metaphysics. Reich will later say that Freud was 'very much dissatisfied genitally' from an unhappy marriage and also that the conservatism of the psychoanalytic movement forced him, in old age, to let the original libido theory be destroyed.

Whatever it is that brings this ghoulish mood, Freud develops his idea of the **DEATH INSTINCT.**

The idea here is that the Nervous System wants to eliminate sensations in order to remain at rest. In short, you desire something in order to stop wanting it, like scratching an itch. Follow this to its extreme and the best way to get rid of feelings is to shuffle off this mortal coil altogether. Human beings seek, by repeating earlier experiences, to return to a state of non-existence or death.

LIFE BECOMES A CONSTANT BATTLE BETWEEN EROS (Love or Life-Force) AND THANATOS (Death)

FREUD would have felt justified had he lived in our mushroom-clouded times, looked over by death dealers and seeming very much like a collective Death Wish.

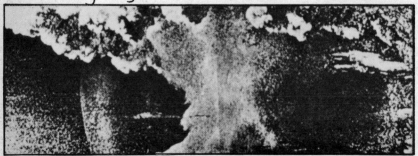

...THAT SOUNDS LIKE ORIGINAL SIN ALL OVER AGAIN, HERR DOKTOR...

Reich is a product of a more positive tradition. In the line of Jean-Jacques Rousseau he believes that people are born innocent and only later corrupted by society.

ROUSSEAU

In 1932 he declares war on the Death Instinct. People are not born perverse and irrational, as the Old Man seems to believe. They are made like that when deprived of SATISFACTION.

INHIBITED SEXUAL ENERGY TURNS INTO DESTRUCTIVE ENERGY.

Even masochists are seeking pleasure like everyone else, but fear of being punished turns them away from satisfaction, and forces them to behave irrationally.

55

Aggression and sadism come from a poor SEX ECONOMY. Just as the economy of a country implies the way it uses its resources and brings about a healthy and vigorous life, so the body's health is determined by the amount of sexual energy released in orgasm.

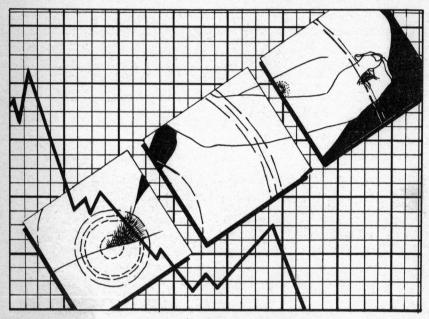

If the body's resources are not properly used, then Energy remains trapped in the body and leads to DEPRESSION, RECESSION, ECONOMIC COLLAPSE and deviant behaviour towards other people.

Not only that. For Reich to accept the Death
Instinct would mean throwing away his
political beliefs. For Freud:

He's full of hope. And why not? Soviet social legislation immediately after the Revolution has been very progressive. In December, 1917, Lenin has issued two decrees on marriage, giving women the right to determine their own sexual and economic life, to decide which name to use, where to live, etc. On paper, at least, it spelled out the beginning of the end of male domination.

Divorce becomes as easy as obtaining mutual consent among the partners. No reason given. Simple as that.

The Soviet authorities try to stop back-street abortions by making state abortions more accessible. More important is the attempt to prevent abortion through propaganda for the use of contraceptives. Special trains are sent to the provinces filled with birth control information and equipment.

Child-care centres take this burden off women soon after birth. Working women are paid for time off during pregnancy and for nursing.

The old Tsarist legislation against homosexuality is eliminated.

A train fitted out as a mobile school to tour remote districts of the Soviet Union. A photograph taken in the early 1920s.

Most important for Reich are the developing attitudes towards bringing up children. He imagines that the commune will replace the authoritarian-patriarchal family unit. In the early years of the revolution children are given the right to openly criticise their parents without fear of punishment...

(Agit prop Train)

But not so fast, Herr Doktor. This is 1929, after all.

This man is in power and has brought all his Character Armour with him. All the progressive work of the past decade is being reversed.

In the young people's communes things are taking a bad turn.

Later on, in 1934, Reich will hear of mass arrests of homosexuals in the major Russian cities, and in the same year a law will be approved explicitly forbidding sexual relations between men.

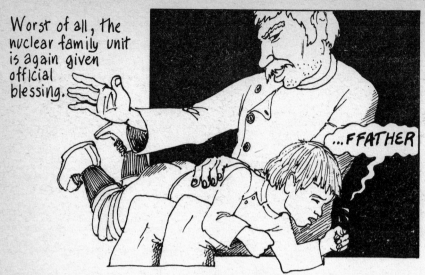

Worst of all, the nuclear family unit is again given official blessing.

...FFATHER

Yet it would be wrong to blame these reactionary developments on the new political changes taking place in the Soviet Union. Reich is quick to understand there have been problems from the very start of the Revolution.

THE REVOLUTION IN THE CULTURAL SUPERSTRUCTURE FAILS TO TAKE PLACE BECAUSE THE BEARER AND GUARDIAN OF THIS REVOLUTION, THE **PSYCHIC STRUCTURE OF HUMAN BEINGS,** HAS NOT CHANGED

Pretty much in common with Dr Freud, the Soviet leaders (including Lenin to some extent) believe sexuality to be incompatible with culture, which here means CLASS STRUGGLE.

Others seem to believe that if you change the economic basis of society, human relationships will change by themselves. Reich now knows better than that.

IT IS EXACTLY THE **PERSONAL LIFE** OF PEOPLE WHICH MUST BE **THE BASIS** OF ANY REVOLUTIONARY MOVEMENT. WE WANT GENITALLY HAPPY PEOPLE, NOT EMOTIONAL CRIPPLES BLINDLY FOLLOWING EVERYTHING STALIN SAYS.

The bureaucrats are not the only ones he doesn't trust.

> WATCH OUT FOR REACTIONARY SOCIAL HYGIENISTS AND PARTY-LINE GYNECOLOGISTS.
> ...**DON'T** TRUST THE EXPERTS, TRUST **YOURSELVES**

The sexual future has to be taken into the hands of the workers and peasants themselves, the stuff of the revolution – especially the young. Sexual happiness is too important to be left to old men...

Just compare the age of the first young revolutionary leaders with the modern Politburo (average age 70), that tells you all you need to know about the development of the Soviet 'Revolution'...

Reich comes away from the Soviet Union with a series of proposals which he later makes in his book...

THE SEXUAL REVOLUTION

1. Prohibit any literature, film, etc. which causes sexual anxiety.
2. Manufacture contraceptives with the same care given to machines, making sure to take them out of the hands of profiteers.
3. Emphasise contraception in the prevention of abortion.
4. Create emergency homes for young people to make love in.
5. Include women in the army and navy so as to avoid the punishment of homosexuality in the military!

Above all he comes away with an idea which will carry him all his life: LEGAL PROTECTION FOR ADOLESCENT AND INFANT SEXUALITY.

The bitterness of his Soviet experience causes him to write:

The sexual resignation which characterises the overwhelming majority of people means indolence, emptiness in life, paralysis of all healthy activity and initiative, or brutal, sadistic excesses; but at the same time it provides a relative calm in life. It is as if death were already anticipated in the way of living

As long as authoritarian governments create PLEASURE ANXIETY in people, they will give up on life and become simply sheep. Very soon, in Germany, he will see his thought come to full and horrible flower...

But he is not without hope. He's got a fight on his hands. But he can't carry it out in the already reactionary Soviet Union or in the claustrophobic and inbred psychoanalytic circles of Vienna. In 1930, there's only one place for a man of his vision to plant his feet.

He heads straight for the dynamic heart of the European experience: BERLIN.

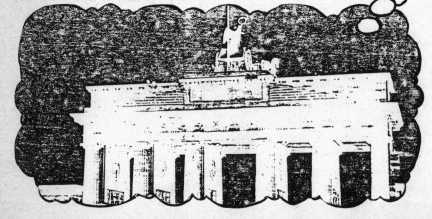

Berlin is not only a thriving centre of culture and new ideas, it is by nature a more progressive town than Vienna. In 1919, after the collapse of the monarchy and establishment of a Republic, there are massive street demonstrations in Berlin.

The Spartakist revolutionary leaders Rosa Luxemburg and Karl Liebknecht are brutally murdered by reactionary soldiers. But small patches of revolutionary activity continue throughout Germany — primarily in Bavaria.

Sooner or later the ruling Social Democrats call in their ultra-right-wing henchmen and bring the German Revolution to a bloody end...

GROSZ Cartoon on 'Frei Korps' savagery.

Snark International

The Social Democrats manage to hold on to their power throughout the 1920's, despite rampaging inflation. But they are strongly challenged on the left by the Communist Party (KPD) and from the right by the National Socialists (Nazis). In 1930, the Communists are still strong, able to call on millions of working-class votes. This is the second largest Communist Party in Europe and the most likely to succeed.

Die große Absäge.

Nazi election poster ⚑ ⚑ Anti-KPD cartoon by Social Democrats (1925)

ARBEITER

WÄHLT DEN FRONTSOLDATEN

HITLER!

'Workers! Vote for the front soldier Hitler!'

After all, the Soviet Union is getting more and more isolated, and needs some support. More important, many look to the KPD as the only force capable of stopping this guy:

It's the perfect spot for WR to find his feet. Away from Freud he can try to integrate his psychoanalytic work with his politics. Even the medical profession and the Berlin psychiatrists are, on the whole, more political than those in Vienna. What's more, they seem to like WR's Orgasm Theory.

Our man doesn't waste a minute. With the agreement of the KPD he sets up another of those longwinded but very much to-the-point institutions. It's called the GERMAN ASSOCIATION FOR PROLETARIAN SEXUAL POLITICS and soon has 20,000 members.

In 1931 he starts the famous VERLAG FÜR SEXUALPOLITIK (SexPol) where he publishes both practical and theoretical sex-political pamphlets.

Here he tries to merge his two areas of work, psychoanalysis and Marxism. It's not easy, especially since advocates of each tend to spit fire at one another. But he gives it a try.

EVERY SOCIAL ORDER CREATES THOSE CHARACTER FORMS WHICH IT NEEDS FOR ITS PRESERVATION

Marx had argued that the ruling class always makes sure its ideology is the ideology of all members of society. It does this through propaganda and through education and by controlling channels of information. Reich takes it further:

IT IS A MATTER OF A DEEP-REACHING PROCESS IN EACH NEW GENERATION, OF THE FORMATION OF A PSYCHIC STRUCTURE WHICH CORRESPONDS TO THE EXISTING SOCIAL ORDER IN ALL STRATA OF THE POPULATION

What's he saying? Basically, not only ideas, but emotions are determined by social factors. Marx believes that Capitalism, for instance, can determine our ideas. To this, Reich adds the unconscious. The ruling ideology can even get into our impulses and our dreams... Watch out!

But Reich's Party work is not just theoretical.

The success of day-to-day organising is very important to him.

WHY ARE WE DOING THIS ON SUCH A BEAUTIFUL DAY?

SLAM!

PLANT SOCIALISATION IN THE SOVIET UNION

KPD

TODAY RUSSIAN COLLECTIVISM

REDS!

RÖTFRONT MARSCH

!

Reich sees the Fascists winning over masses of working-class people.

He comes up with a series of proposals for the Party:

☆ No manipulating or spellbinding the masses. Be concrete and direct.

☆ Don't ask people to do more than they can carry out.
Work slowly and progressively.

☆ Politicise all the trivial aspects of daily life: the dance hall, the cinema, the grocery, the bedroom, the pub, the bookies
—That's where the energy of the revolution is!

☆ No boring leaflets, please!

☆ No heroes. No martyrs. Conserve your energies.

☆ Remember that cops are working-class men.

☆ Free time for Party functionaries.

☆ Don't cower before authority. Just imagine a cop standing around in his underpants!

When Reich arrives in 1930, he finds about 80 different sex-political groups in Germany, as well as many birth control centres, often infiltrated by shady contraceptive dealers.

His idea is to unite them all in his Sex-Pol organisation, under the umbrella of the KPD. What are their demands?

1. better housing conditions for the masses.
2. abolition of laws against abortion and homosexuality.
3. alteration of marriage and divorce laws.
4. free birth control advice and contraceptives.
5. health protection for mothers and children.
6. nurseries in factories and work-places
7. abolition of laws prohibiting sex education.
8. home leave for prisoners.

BUT... THESE LIBERALS ARE ALL MIDDLE-AGED AND HAVE **NO** *YOUTH PROGRAMME.* WE'LL HAVE TO CHANGE THAT...

Just what goes on in these Sex-Political centres anyway?

For Reich, that depends on the problems people bring to him. Above all he's out to fight problems of bourgeois morality among working-class people.

ONLY THROUGH SOCIALISM CAN YOU ACHIEVE SEXUAL 'JOIE DE VIVRE'

DOKTOR; WE WELCOME ECONOMIC AND SEXUAL INDEPENDENCE OF WOMEN. BUT...THERE IS A CONTRADICTION BETWEEN THIS AND A GENUINE DESIRE TO BE A MOTHER

WE CAN'T SOLVE THAT ONE UNDER CAPITALISM. ONLY WHEN SOCIALISM SEPARATES THE ECONOMIC FUNCTION FROM THE SEXUAL ONE WILL WOMEN BE ABLE TO WORK THROUGH THIS DILEMMA

WOMEN IN THE PARTY TELL ME IT'S WRONG TO WEAR MAKE UP AND BEAUTIFUL CLOTHES. THEY SAY IT'S 'BOURGEOIS', BUT I LIKE TO LOOK GOOD.

Reich sees the Party's Puritanism as an affront to many women who, given the money, would strive to look beautiful. This denies a healthy vanity in most human beings.

WE MUST FIND A COMPROMISE BETWEEN BOURGEOIS GLAMOUR AND COMMUNIST ASCETICISM.

On the question of children, he doesn't (and never will) mince words

SAY 'THANK YOU' TO THE GENTLEMAN

...IDEOLOGICAL STRUGGLE AGAINST 'BEING GOOD' IS A VITAL POLITICAL TASK

- Struggle against compulsive toilet training.

- Any parent seen beating a child in public should be challenged.

- No interfering with infantile sexuality or masturbation.

It also disturbs Reich that small children are drifting to Hitler, being encouraged by war games and war toys.

There is something to it, some satisfaction, some increased self-confidence in holding a weapon, in marching to rhythm.

It's reactionary and regrettable, but we had better start understanding it — and fast.

CRITIQUE#2

One of Reich's wives, Ilse Ollendorff, reports that Reich 'always insisted with great strictness on good behaviour and proper table manners in public places', and was very 'annoyed' when his own children 'misbehaved'. His relations with his daughters, from all the available evidence, was strained.

As for his son, Peter, who served the U.S. military machine against the people of Indo-China and whose childhood memories seem well-peppered with guns (W.R. also liked the feel of a gun in his hand), he had this to say:

'I'm sorry he (Reich) gave me an attitude toward military authority that was consistent with his paternity... but inconsistent with his philosophy'

Reich's main emphasis is on the teenagers.

They need rooms of their own to make love in. Who can help them out here? The Communist Party, of course. Yet the Party is doing very badly at recruiting youth...

Hitler does it much better. Why?
Isn't Fascism rigidly authoritarian and anti-sexual?

This is also the reason why most adolescents join the Party's youth organisations in the first place: to find a sexual partner or two or three. The Party's official morality rejects this view. The result: young people drift away, many of them over to the Nazis.
The Party had better take account of their personal lives.

Reich writes his pamphlet 'The Sexual Struggle of Youth'. It gives concrete advice on masturbation, orgasm, birth control and claims that sexual satisfaction is a primary aim of socialism. This is destined to get up the noses of Party bureaucrats. The Nazis will eventually get round to dealing with WR's books, but the KPD is even quicker in silencing this 'pornography'.

CRITIQUE#3

In his later years, Reich will attempt to play down the significance of his political work.

Some of his idolatrous followers – including his posthumous editors – go as far as to say 'he was never politically oriented', as if there were some terrible stigma attached to the idea.

Reich's later hatred of Communists (he will call them Red Fascists) is very understandable considering his treatment at their hands. But this bitterness will cloud the great importance of his political work.

His analysis of social and political events brings a programme for more efficient and more humane left-wing parties. More important, as we are about to see, he understands why the Party, when it fails to respond to personal needs, is destroyed in 1933 when it has a real chance to win power...

WHILE WE PRESENTED THE MASSES WITH HISTORICAL ANALYSES AND ECONOMIC TREATISES ON THE CONTRADICTIONS OF IMPERIALISM, HITLER STIRRED THE DEEPEST ROOTS OF THEIR EMOTIONAL BEING

Reich is formally expelled from the KPD in 1933, but this doesn't stop him from doing political work in Germany. A more immediate cause is the smell of smoke on February 28, 1933.

The Reichstag fire leads to the arrest of thousands of left-wing functionaries.

Also, 'The Sexual Struggle of Youth' has come to the attention of the Völkischer Beobachter, a Nazi paper. It's time to go...

Book burning by Nazi students.

REICH SENDS HIS CHILDREN OFF TO VIENNA, AND...

...AFTER A FEW DAYS OF HANGING OUT IN HOTELS UNDER FALSE NAMES,

HE SLIPS THROUGH THE BORDER INTO **AUSTRIA** IN MARCH 1933

Like many others, though, he hopes it's all temporary. March 5, 1933 is election day in Germany. Forty thousand workers, many armed, wait for spontaneous demonstrations which will stop Hitler from taking power... but

HINDENBURG WELCOMES THE NEW CHANCELLOR HITLER

THE LEFT CAPITULATES THIS IS ASTONISHING.

Just why have so many millions of workers gone over to Hitler against their own interests?

BECAUSE HITLER WAS PAID BY THE CAPITALISTS

BECAUSE THE SOCIAL DEMOCRATS SOLD OUT THE WORKERS

BECAUSE OF STALIN!

There are other historical and economic reasons: By 1931 there are over 7 million unemployed in Germany.

The country has suffered a crisis of national identity after defeat in the first war; the economic humiliations forced on it by the winning powers create an atmosphere ripe for a resurgence of nationalism.

Reich is watching the events from a different vantage point. He asks some curious questions:

> HOW COULD THE GERMAN WORKERS IN JANUARY, 1934 ACCEPT THE DRACONIAN ANTI-LABOUR LEGISLATION INTRODUCED BY THE NAZIS?

> WHY IS IT THAT POVERTY-STRICKEN PEOPLE SHOW SUCH SELF-CONTROL?

> WHY HAD MILLIONS OF GERMAN WOMEN VOTED **AGAINST** THE ABOLITION OF THE LAW WHICH FORBIDS ABORTION?

> WHY, IN NOVEMBER 1919, WHEN THE WORKERS WERE DEMONSTRATING IN THE BERLIN TIERGARTEN, DID THEY TAKE CARE **NOT** TO WALK ON THE GRASS?

Why, in short, do people NOT rebel?

> ...IT'S VERBOTEN

> THE WORKING CLASS HAS BEEN SUCCESSFULLY **BOURGEOISIFIED**

But that's not the whole story.
Reich is increasingly impressed by the Nazis' mass psychological methods. But his warnings are not taken seriously by the Communist Party who see Hitler as a lackey of finance capital and nothing more. They expect him to soon fade away.

Reich recognises some progressive elements in the midst of fascism's ultra reactionary ideology. The result of his analysis is his most important book, THE MASS PSYCHOLOGY OF FASCISM (1934).

Annual Party Rally in Nuremberg, 1934.

Reich sees Hitler as the culmination of centuries of human oppression under patriarchy.

To the questions he raises, he answers that masses of people, moving AGAINST THEM-SELVES in bringing their enemies to power, have acted IRRATIONALLY. (Later he will come to believe that ALL politics is irrational!)

IN ITS PURE FORM FASCISM IS THE SUM TOTAL OF ALL THE IRRATIONAL REACTIONS OF THE AVERAGE HUMAN CHARACTER

The Madhouse, by Goya, c. 1800

The Nazis' biggest emotional tool is fear...

"GREY DAY" Painting by GROSZ

Their real power base is among the lower middle class who fear they will lose their small gains and fall back into economic misery again. This is a real possibility in the inflation-plagued Weimar Republic. Hitler has to pretend to be against Big Business in order to win their support.

This class is also traditionally terrified of disorder. Reich observes them identifying with authority, accepting without question the role of police, the military, the State. This tradition is well recognised and exploited by most modern right-wing politicians.

But Hitler's greatest trick is undoubtedly the RACE THEORY. By turning the Jews into capitalists and money lenders, he channels people's fear of economic deprivation. Reich takes it further: the Jews also become the object of in-grained sexual anxiety. The Race Theory compensates for the German people's terrible sexual and moral self-image, which has taken a beating in the Big War and in the Depression of the 1920's.

The promise to maintain the 'purity of blood' plays on the very real fear of SYPHILIS at the time. The Jewish religious practice of circumcision intensifies unconscious CASTRATION ANXIETY.

But unlike those leftists who merely dismiss the perverse Nazi theories, Reich understands that the fear of 'pollution and contamination of emotional life' is not a fantasy, but very real indeed and not to be ignored. The Nazis also know all the tricks of military performance, marches and rallies (just look at the incredibly choreographed Nuremberg rallies).

THE SEXUAL EFFECT OF A UNIFORM, THE EROTICALLY PROVOCATIVE EFFECT OF RHYTHMICALLY EXECUTED GOOSE-STEPPING, THE EXHIBITIONISTIC NATURE OF MILITARISTIC PROCEDURES, HAVE BEEN MORE PRACTICALLY COMPREHENDED BY A SALESGIRL OR AVERAGE SECRETARY THAN BY OUR MOST ERUDITE POLITICIANS

LT. W. REICH
1917

SPORT too, especially FOOTBALL 'has a directly depoliticising effect and encourages the reactionary tendencies of youth'. (Witness the English football grounds on a Saturday afternoon; or poor Argentinians parading their World Cup through the streets for days on end to bolster the fascist dictatorship which tortured, impoverished and dehumanised them).

All these things — football, rallies, marches, excitation over heroes and leaders, slogan-shouting, even the sentimentality to be found in the 'behaviour of the audience at a third-rate musical' (a pastime exploited by the Nazis) are all enforced alternatives to a HEALTHY SEX LIFE.

Fascism is the 'basic emotional attitude of the suppressed man of our authoritarian machine civilisation and its mechanical-mystical conception of life'

The State maintains POWER by assuring the 'atrophy of the sexual apparatus' through compulsive morality and that all-time number one favourite SELF-CONTROL

All of this leads to the building of protective character armour, a turning-off of the orgastic tap and – in the end – PARALYSIS OF THE WILL TO REBEL

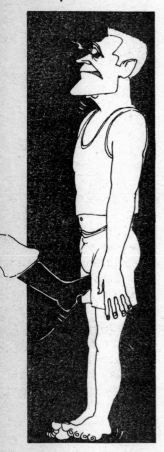

Heil!

In short, if you make people fear their genitals, they will fear the world. It was inevitable that Reich would answer his curious questions within the framework of his own Orgasm Theory. Sexual inhibition and fear cause people to think and act against their own emotional interests.

But people are not born this way. They don't begin life not wanting to be FREE.

How does it begin?

WHY ARE THE NAZIS SO KEEN ON MOTHERS PRODUCING BABIES FOR THE FATHERLAND?

The Fascists — and WR — know that the authoritarian pattern begins inside THE FAMILY. Obeying and adoring the Führer really begins with obeying and adoring Father.

The Nazis naturally beef up the image of the German Family, relegating women to the role of broody hens.

Their children will most likely be the victims of their parents' own fears, and their chief weapon against them will be GENITAL SUPPRESSION...

The Family – as we have seen – is a 'factory for authoritarian ideologies'.

In the first four or five years of life the child is forced to adapt to society as he will find it outside the home.

Teenagers are fed marriage propaganda and the lie that sexuality is a by-product of procreation

NOW THEY CAN GET ON WITH THE MARITAL OBLIGATIONS RACKET...

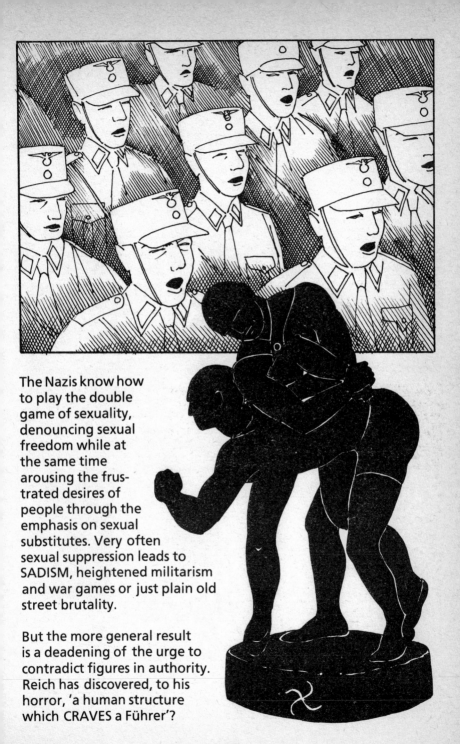

The Nazis know how to play the double game of sexuality, denouncing sexual freedom while at the same time arousing the frustrated desires of people through the emphasis on sexual substitutes. Very often sexual suppression leads to SADISM, heightened militarism and war games or just plain old street brutality.

But the more general result is a deadening of the urge to contradict figures in authority. Reich has discovered, to his horror, 'a human structure which CRAVES a Führer'?

His answer to it, on a mass scale, is not much different from his therapeutic answer, one to one, in the Vienna Clinic: "PEOPLE MUST BE ACTIVELY ENCOURAGED TO GOVERN THEIR OWN DESTINIES". This means a long and tough process of unlearning all the checks on freedom instilled by family and State.

Reich had hoped that the yearnings of people could be given REAL expression — (as opposed to the MYSTICAL expression of the Nazis) by the vanguard Communist Party.

When that fails, he toys momentarily with the idea of a new party.

But very soon he finds himself damning parties altogether.

HELP YOURSELF AND FIGHT FOR THE MEANS TO ENABLE YOU TO HELP YOURSELF

DO NOT BEG FOR LIBERTY AND BREAD; DO NOT ACCEPT THEM FROM ECONOMIC OPPRESSORS OR POLITICAL PIRATES.

Now begins WR's exile not only from the country of his best work, but from his friends, his language and, sooner or later, from his two most important concerns: Marxism and psychoanalysis.

It's 1934. Hitler is firmly entrenched in power.

Even many communists, including workers' para-military squads, are going over to Hitler.

Reich publishes his MASS PSYCHOLOGY OF FASCISM to demonstrate why. The first line of the book:

The German working-class has suffered severe defeat...

But the Party and the Comintern deny it, even now...

THIS IS 'MERELY A TRANSITORY DEFEAT IN THE COURSE OF REVOLUTIONARY PROGRESS'

Reich moves to Denmark, that sleepy, low blood-pressured country bordering Germany, a natural haven for many exiles.

He wants to set up shop as a practising analyst. He asks the Psychoanalytical Association for permission.

NEIN HE'S A BOLSHEVIK.

He tries to do sex-political work.

NOT FOR US. HE'S A FREUDIAN

HE HAS DISPLAYED UN-COMMUNIST AND ANTI-PARTY BEHAVIOUR, AND WRITTEN A COUNTERREVOLUTIONARY BOOK (MASS PSYCHOLOGY)

HE IS THEREFORE EXPELLED FROM THE DANISH COMMUNIST PARTY

He tries to stay in Denmark, but...

In Germany the Nazis don't care much for him either...

We know where those will end up:

Reich moves across the Sound to Malmo in southern Sweden.

He gives sex-political and psychoanalytic training to a group of students.

But right away the gossip starts.

Who is this strange doctor with his SEX-POL?

AND WHAT IS THIS PSYCHOANALYSIS ANYWAY?

PEOPLE ARE FOLLOWING ME. THEY'RE BORED. IN A SMALL TOWN LIKE THIS, THAT LEADS TO FASCISM...

Here we go again. In May, 1934 Reich gets thrown out of Sweden...

And that's not all. In August 1934 he goes to the Congress of the International Psychoanalytic Association in Lucerne. The entire Freudian mafia is there.

REICH HAS BEEN EXPELLED FROM THE ASSOCIATION...

So now he's lost his second home. Everywhere he's in disgrace.

REICH IS A PARANOID...

Who wouldn't be? Where can he go now? In Germany they'd lock him up – or worse. The Nazis have their eyes on his native Austria and anyway that's where the Freudians hang out. Denmark and Sweden have kicked him out. He doesn't care much for Paris; and London...

WELL ... IT'S ALL SO RIGID THERE FULLY ARMOURED

THEY EVEN TOILET-TRAIN THEIR CHILDREN AT SIX MONTHS TO MAKE THEM 'CAPABLE OF CULTURE'

No, the less said about England the better (although what country on Earth would ever have more need of him!)

In October 1934 (what a year!) he moves to Oslo, Norway, and manages to stay there for five years.

In 1936 he founds yet another of those institutes, this one for SEX-ECONOMIC BIORESEARCH to study the use of sexual energy.

WAIT A MINUTE. WHERE DID **BIORESEARCH** COME FROM?

Well, WR's political work is more or less at an end. His contact with outside groups has been cut off. His work is becoming very private and exclusively scientific. He might have been going this way in any case. But losing his bases in both the Party and psychoanalysis has brought to a quick close the most socially useful part of his life. From now on he's going to get far away from helping large numbers of people.

In Norway he gets back to Character Analysis. But now this has developed into something he calls

VEGETOTHERAPY

This is a true break with Freud because the analyst is no longer a passive observer listening to words words words. Also, for Freud, who seems to have no real interest in the patient's body, there has been a strict taboo against touching the patient. Not for WR...

Early character analysis was meant to give the patient an objective view of his own character armour, very much as traditional psychoanalysis discloses the source of a neurotic symptom by associative talking. Now Reich is going further. He's after the MUSCLES.

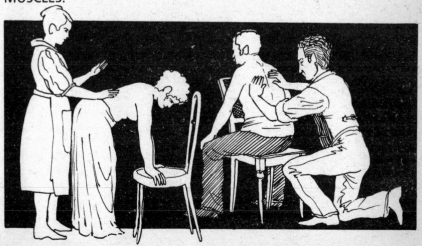

With Vegetotherapy Reich is getting close to Psychosomatic Medicine. The idea is that muscular rigidities in the body contain the history of their origin.

We've already seen how an authoritarian family can imprint its repressions on a child...

Reich believes these turn into character traits and are expressed through muscular tension which is a more direct way of saying 'character armour'.

THESE RIGID MUSCLES, IN EFFECT, HOLD REPRESSED EMOTIONS

Reich can see these repressions in the way a patient moves, sits, talks, etc.

It's time to get to work loosening those tense muscles. But it means touching the patient, perhaps even aggressively, and getting some aggression in return...

HOW
DOES
IT
WORK
?

He starts by releasing the anxiety around the eyes.

The eyelids are a major source of tension.

This leads to the mouth and chin to release feelings of anger and sometimes disgust.

MANY PEOPLE HAVE A MASK-LIKE FACIAL EXPRESSION.

LET'S WORK ON THAT.

Reich is working downward because he believes that energy flows up and down along the body axis.

This brings him to the neck and shoulders, which usually hold back anger or crying.

Just think about how you can see tears swallowed down by watching the Adam's apple.

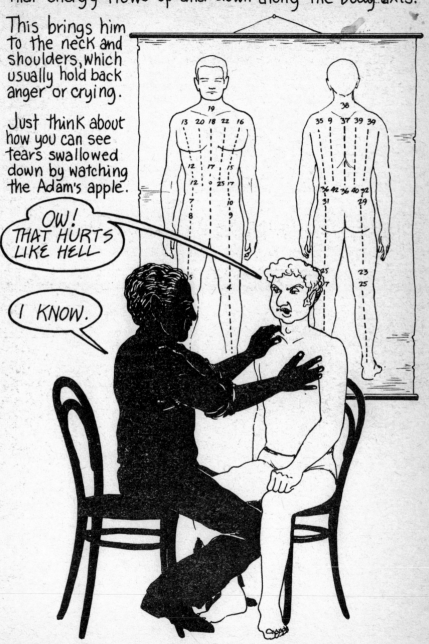

OW! THAT HURTS LIKE HELL

I KNOW.

As he goes along, Reich emphasises the importance of breathing technique.

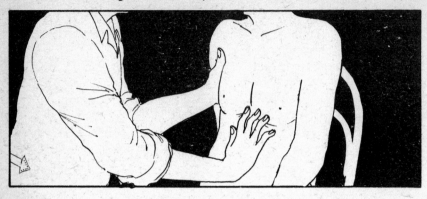

Our famous SELF-CONTROL is usually managed through a constriction of the breathing apparatus in the chest. It's also a way of effectively killing pleasure in the body.

Where is this all leading?
To the groin of the matter, of course. The goal of
Vegetotherapy is a full-blooded, unrestricted
ORGASM REFLEX.

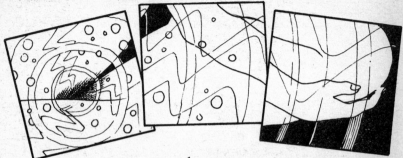

At the end of the therapy (it can take years) Reich works on
the rigid pelvis which holds a great deal of anger and anxiety.

He achieves full breathing and then a shimmying of the
buttocks begins. The muscular release now is meant to
simulate orgasm in therapy. Presumably, the suppressed
emotions are discharged this way.

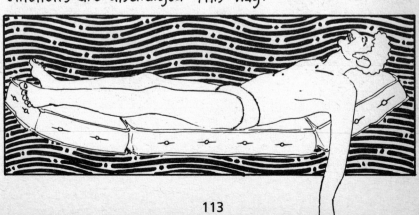

This of course is the ideal. Mostly Reich concentrates on those areas of the body chiefly afflicted with rigidity. By constantly calling it to the patient's attention and working on the area, the rigidity is loosened. This can be accompanied, as in traditional psychoanalysis, by a recall of the trauma which led to the rigid area in the first place.

But Reich is not content to stop his work there. He wants to go deeper and deeper into the question of sexual energy which has always obsessed him.

In keeping with his emphasis on scientific FACT, he is determined to prove that the orgasm is a MATERIAL THING, that the sexual energy (libido) is verifiable and can be MEASURED.

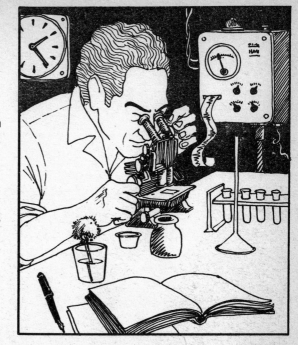

Reich points out that changes in the electrical potential of the skin as a result of emotions can be measured in something called the 'psychogalvanic phenomenon'.

But how do we go about measuring amounts of sexual pleasure?

115

He sets up a series of experiments with students and colleagues in Oslo...

THIS SHOWS A WAVE-LIKE OSCILLATION, THE 'TICKLING PHENOMENON'. TICKLING IS A VARIANT OF SEXUAL FRICTION.

Reich concludes that the erogenous zones – lips, anus, nipples, penis, mucus membrane of the vagina, earlobe, tongue, palms and FOREHEAD – react much more strongly than other parts of the skin. This apparently shows in his instruments.

But you don't even need to be directly connected. For example:

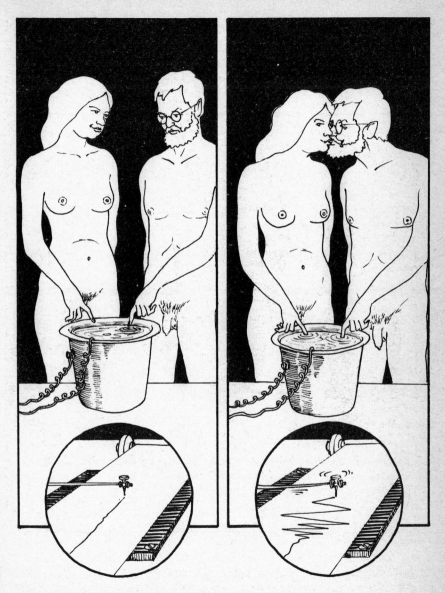

The reaction of course increases with stroking of hands and so on, presumably right up to the ULTIMATE STROKE.

But if the subject doesn't like being touched, for instance, this results in a decrease or UN-PLEASURE REACTION. Emotionally blocked or muscularly rigid subjects show a negative reaction.

In fact, all emotions associated with unpleasure, like pain, fear, anxiety, depression, etc...

'are accompanied by a decrease in surface charge of the organism'. Death or dying results in a heavily decreased charge and finally the ENERGY SOURCE IS EXTINGUISHED.

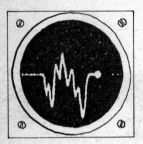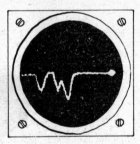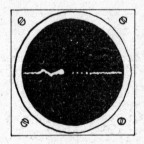

What does all this mean? It means that Reich thinks he's taken Freud's idea of LIBIDO and proved it is part of a general electric process in nature. Orgasm has become a bioelectrical discharge, followed by mechanical relaxation in the body...

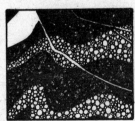

But why stop there. If this works in humans, why not in all living things?

From the formula he sees working in the orgasm, Reich claims that 'the life process is determined by a four beat rhythm':

Well, we can see how that might work as a theory for the function of orgasm, but does it really solve the mystery of life? Reich thinks so.

THESE ARE CHARGED WITH BIOLOGICAL ENERGY.

Reich calls these particles BIONS. After further study he claims these are transformed into microbes. In effect, it would mean life can be born from inanimate organic matter. Most scientists believe this to be impossible and say that all living cells can only derive from other cells. Needless to say, Reich's discoveries are not taken seriously by the scientific establishment. But he is used to that by now.

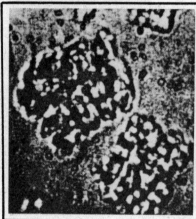
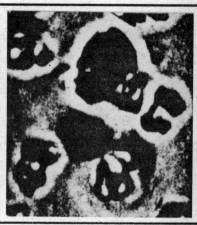

'Bion-Vesicles.'

There's no stopping him now. He discovers that BIONS give off a kind of blue radiation. He calls this ORGONE ENERGY, and believes he has made a discovery which will change the entire face of biology. Later he calls this LIFE ENERGY, (or Le, since he begins to initialise everything) and this is exactly what he has been LOOKING FOR all along.

Time for another... # CRITICAL INTERRUPTION

This is the point at which most of his critics say Reich goes mad, even those who believe he's done great work before 1934. And surely his paranoia and obsessions are increasing.
He loses friends and colleagues like strands of hair because he's impossible to work with, dictatorial, irritable.

About this time Reich recounts a dream/daydream for some friends: he's riding into Berlin as a conquering hero on a white horse, with Ravel's Bolero playing in the background

What is WR actually up to? He's discovering the SOURCE OF LIFE and giving its components made-up names or initials.
He's more and more withdrawn from the world. Either his discoveries are correct and 99% of all previous science pure rubbish, or WR is preparing his election to the post of God.

In any case, the Norwegians have had enough of him too. In 1937, a slanderous newspaper campaign against him begins, and gets worse when he starts talking publicly about BIONS.

The Norwegian medical establishment isn't too happy about WR letting slip that he's working on a cancer cure. Who knows what sets it off.

By this time, he's a permanent exile and a man on the run, chasing himself (and being chased) deeper and deeper into a martyr's role.

But he's not giving up. There's still one 'life-affirmative' door left open to him, where he feels his work will be welcomed. He's had enough of the stifling European atmosphere...

In 1939, just a few days before Hitler blows the lid off the Old World, Reich steps off the boat into the New one.

America is just the ticket. Reich will never have to leave this place or be kicked out. He even becomes a citizen and gung-ho American patriot.

He also finds just the right climate for his work. Even conservative Americans are more liberal and open-minded than those stale Europeans, he thinks, wishfully.

He hasn't quite discovered yet that their wide-eyed interest in what he's doing is part of a broad welcome to nearly every charlatan who's got a new trick to show off. But never mind that now. He's about to introduce his fellow Americans to...

125

THE ORGONE

And just what is this ORGONE?

The word derives from a combination of 'organism' and 'orgasm'. It's something like the idea of ELAN VITAL, except of course that it is more concrete than that. It is the energy of all living organisms and material, and it is the motor force of the ORGASM REFLEX which for Reich, is always the key to HEALTH.

What are it's
properties?

Orgone is blue
and can be seen,
for example,
in the bluish
colouration
of frogs
about to mate

It can be
measured
with an
electroscope,
a
Geiger Counter
or an
Orgone Energy
Field Meter

It's present
EVERYWHERE
in space
and in vacuums.

Gravity,
electromagnetism
and light,
all function
through
the medium of
ORGONE

ALL LIVING MATTER IS CREATED FROM THIS ENERGY

Originally, Reich perceives orgone as being a unique energy source of life, but in 1951 he decides that ALL MATERIAL REALITY comes from it.

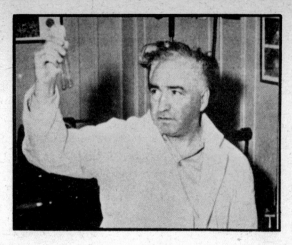

So that all activities in space - hurricanes, cyclones, sunspots, even tidal movements and other aspects of weather— are caused by the 'Superimposition' of several cosmic energy systems.

The human equivalent is Coitus, where two separate energy systems 'superimpose' (often producing a third!)

In short, Orgone Energy is pretty much EVERYTHING.

What we call 'heat waves' in the air have nothing to do with heat; that's Orgone shimmering there. The atmospheric movements which annoy astronomers looking through telescopes; that's no atmospheric disturbance, that's Orgone. What we call 'static' in the air has nothing to do with electricity; it's ORGONE, blue blue ORGONE...

...THE COLOUR OF LUMINATING, DECAYING WOOD IS BLUE; SO ARE THE LUMINATING TAIL ENDS OF GLOW WORMS, ST. ELMO'S FIRE, AND THE AURORA BOREALIS...

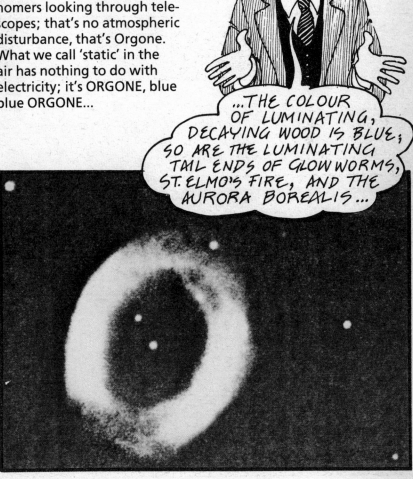

But WR is in the land of practical folks. He's not content with having discovered and measured the source of all existence, he needs to find a way of making it VISIBLE and ACTIVE...

In 1940 he builds the first ORGONE ENERGY ACCUMULATOR (disparagingly called the Orgone Box), a construction he believes will help mankind, but which will soon bring about his downfall.

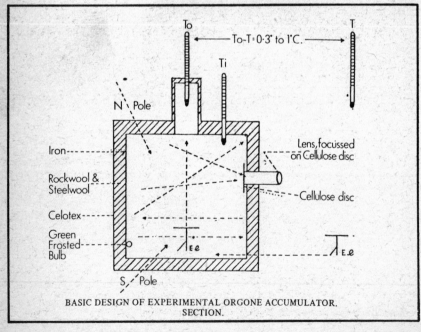

BASIC DESIGN OF EXPERIMENTAL ORGONE ACCUMULATOR.
SECTION.

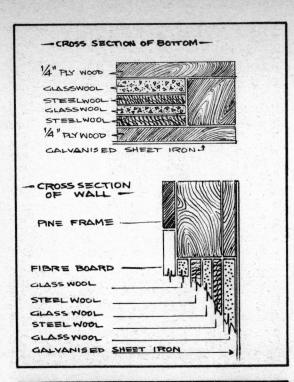

—CROSS SECTION OF BOTTOM—

¼" PLY WOOD
GLASSWOOL
STEELWOOL
GLASSWOOL
STEELWOOL
¼" PLY WOOD
GALVANISED SHEET IRON

→ CROSS SECTION
OF WALL ←

PINE FRAME

FIBRE BOARD
GLASS WOOL
STEEL WOOL
GLASS WOOL
STEEL WOOL
GLASS WOOL
GALVANISED SHEET IRON

The Accumulator is a large box made of organic material (wood, etc) outside, and metal on the inside.

Organic matter is supposed to absorb orgone energy while metal attracts and reflects it.

In this way the energy is directed from the inner walls to the patient who sits inside.

The concentrated Orgone Energy inside affects the biological energy of the human organism, thereby strengthening it and checking any disturbance in the flow of energy.

A patient sits inside for a short time while the healing process takes place.

It can be used for minor wounds or burns and presumably for any illness including cancer. Which is not to say —as some will say— that Reich claims he's got a cancer cure. But many of his patients are terminal cancer victims and he experiments with them and also with cancerous mice.

CANCER IS DUE TO A STAGNATION OF THE FLOW OF LIFE ENERGY IN THE ORGANISM. THE FUNCTION OF THE ACCUMULATOR IS TO GET IT MOVING AGAIN.

By the end of 1940, Reich is so pleased with his discovery that he goes to see no one less than Albert Einstein...

Reich gets no more satisfaction from the Great Man.

In later years he will come to believe this is part of a Communist Conspiracy against him.

WR is becoming more and more isolated.

During the early 1940's he begins to gather a small group of collaborators around him, based on his idea of WORK DEMOCRACY. This is an obvious step after being so badly burned by organisations in his day, and fits very well in his attempt to remake the world in his own image.

He wants no more of parties or bureaucracies. His new idea is that only those who do productive work should govern the world, and each in his own sphere. Farmers determine how land should be farmed, scientists take care of science, street cleaners decide how streets should be cleaned. This is the only hope of preventing a third world war. He creates the slogan:

'LOVE, WORK AND KNOWLEDGE ARE THE WELLSPRINGS OF OUR LIFE. THEY SHOULD ALSO GOVERN IT'

INTERRUPTION

Reich is turning inward now. Work Democracy is a kind of Character Armour which protects him from being further rejected by the outside world. He calls it democracy but will brook no contradiction from his associates. He also creates the WILHELM REICH INFANT TRUST whose first purpose is:

TO SAFEGUARD THE TRUTH ABOUT MY LIFE AND WORK AGAINST DISTORTION AND SLANDER AFTER MY DEATH

All of his documents and papers are to be stored away for fifty years after his death to protect them from 'emotionally sick people who will try to damage my reputation'. Around the same time he begins to oversee English translations of all his books written between 1929-34. Unfortunately for the future, he 'revises' them to accord with his later discovery of the Orgone.

What we read now in English are, in large part, not the original works.

Reich now takes his utopian vision into the countryside around Rangeley in Maine.

He has already established the Orgone Institute and the Orgone Institute Press. Now he establishes ORGONON, home of the Accumulator, and where, eventually, he hopes to set up research hospitals, nurseries, observatories, treatment centres, etc.

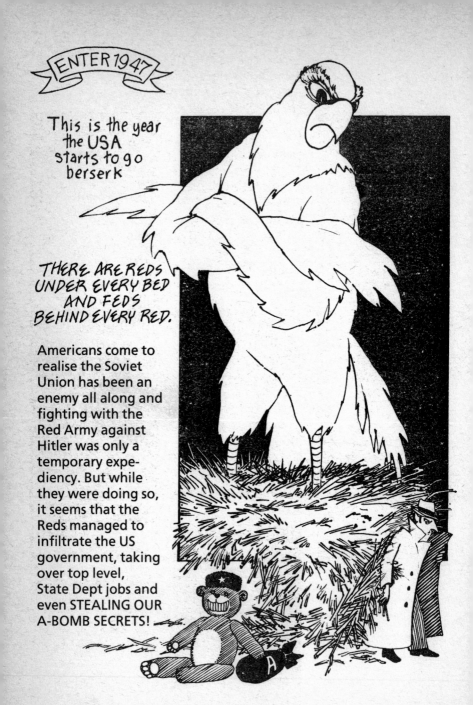

This is the year the USA starts to go berserk

THERE ARE REDS UNDER EVERY BED AND FEDS BEHIND EVERY RED.

Americans come to realise the Soviet Union has been an enemy all along and fighting with the Red Army against Hitler was only a temporary expediency. But while they were doing so, it seems that the Reds managed to infiltrate the US government, taking over top level, State Dept jobs and even STEALING OUR A-BOMB SECRETS!

Lots of politicians make a killing on this new conspiracy idea, the most famous being Senator ←JOE McCARTHY with his laundry lists full of 'names' of spies; and the young Representative from California RICHARD NIXON,

who rises to fame chasing an ex-State Dept. official, ALGER HISS→ into court and eventually prison.

And the so-called 'Atom-Spies' ←ETHEL and JULIUS ROSENBERG will be caught and later fried in the Electric Chair.

The USA is about to start turning out Hydrogen Bombs, and a war-time general who can't pronounce the word 'nuclear' is going to be President.

The time is ripe for a virulent ex-now-anti-Communist like Reich to join in the slurs against 'red Fascists', CP 'snipers' and 'Chinese Red Devils'.

He even proposes a name change for the infamous House Committee on Un-American Activities to the 'Congressional Committee to Safeguard the Process Toward Self-Government'

ONLY THOSE WHO ARE **RIGHT** — LIKE ME — SHOULD FIGHT THE COMMUNISTS.

NOT THOSE WHO OPPOSE SELF-RULE

...WHAT — RULE ?!

What WR doesn't yet grasp is that he, with his Austrian accent and his orgones hidden away in the Maine mountains might also just be an object of suspicion in these days of national paranoia.

Eventually, at Orgonon...

WHO'S THIS COMING UP THE LANE?

...IT'S AN INSPECTOR FOR THE **US** FOOD AND DRUG ADMINISTRATION

WHAT DOES HE WANT?

...I'VE BEEN READING ABOUT THAT THERE ORGONE BOX, MR. REICH...

The bad press is starting again.

They've left him alone for ten years, but now, two liberal magazines, Harpers and the New Republic, have published sensationalist articles claiming 'the Accumulator is being promoted as a cure-all' for cancer and that it can 'enhance sexual potency'

This isn't the last he'll hear from the 'FDA snipers'...

143

Now he's sure of the conspiracy against Orgonomy. It drives him further and further into his work where he finds not only comfort, but his own image writ large. Orgonomy may or may not be based on verifiable scientific principles, but it's very quickly turning into a personal THEOLOGY with WR as Prime Mover...

Like any religion, Orgonomy begins to offer a total universal system with complete internal coherence. Everything fits neatly into it. WR can prove anything he believes.

He thinks that Orgonomy differs from traditional science insofar as it conceives of space as containing moving energy rather than being static and empty. He's moving at breakneck pace away from the human organism (he's tired of treating neurotics) out into the landscape and away into the heavens.

ORGONON IS NOW EQUIPPED WITH A HIGH-POWERED TELESCOPE AND WR MAKES A FEW MORE SENSATIONAL DISCOVERIES:

1. The spiral shape found in the northern lights is explained by two 'superimposed' orgone currents in effect creating a COSMIC ORGASM.

2. Universal gravitation, as science has up to now understood it, does not exist. The stars, the sun and all the planets are 'floating' on an 'ocean' of Orgone.

If this is Theology, then where is God?

Well, WR, once an atheist and dedicated anti-mystic, has found that what we call 'GOD' and what the ancients called 'ether' is all the same as Orgone. 'God' is the effect of man recognising the Cosmic Orgone Ocean...

Jesus Christ is back too. He is THE Genital Character par excellence. He has also become something of a prude.

CHRIST HATED THE DIRTY FUCK OUT OF NOWHERE INTO NOTHINGNESS

146

Reich writes his book,
THE MURDER
OF CHRIST.
Christ's healing
capacity stems from
his powerful energy
field which stimulates
the putrefying energy
fields of the diseased.
But men who are
sick with Character
Armour can't bear
the Life-Affirming
nature of a loving,
orgasmically healthy
being like Christ,
and therefore must
murder him over
and over again
in each generation
and in every aspect
of life.

Children continue to play a vital role in WR's hope for the future. In 1942 and 1952 he sends proposals to the US Congress 'On Laws Needed for the Protection of Life in Newborns and of Truth'.

MY LAWS WILL PROTECT CHILDREN FROM EMOTIONALLY SICK MOTHERS AND OTHER SICK INDIVIDUALS

His laws would also PROSECUTE 'biopathic individuals' for failing to tell children the 'truth'. In the last years, he places children high up near the celestial throne (perhaps on his right side) and dedicates his books to THE CHILD OF THE FUTURE.

ITS EYES SPARKLE WITH A GENTLE GLOW AND LOOK INTO THE WORLD WITH A QUIET, DEEP GAZE. IT IS SOFT IN ITS TOUCH OF HANDS. IT CAN STROKE SO THAT THE STROKED ONE BEGINS TO RADIATE HIS OWN LIFE ENERGY.

There must be a source of Evil in this theological vision. There is. It's called the EMOTIONAL PLAGUE or just E.P. This is the exact opposite of life-affirmative behaviour (like Christ's) and manifests itself irrationally. Once upon a time Reich would have called it Character Armour. But now he's fighting it, not as a neurotic symptom in a sick patient, but a sickness pervading the whole of life.

Sleep of Reason by GOYA.

It becomes for Reich, and for many of his ogling admirers, a means of identifying the enemy.

...HE'S PLAGUEY

149

The Emotional Plague is responsible for the emotional desert that life on Earth has become. Sexual repression has made us sterile. We are suffering a desolation of emotion.

150

But this 'Desert' is not only a metaphor. All around him Reich sees the landscape drying up, trees dying, the rocks 'blackening', devastation everywhere...

Reich, now also referring to himself as the Silent Observer (or SO) begins to recognise this as Deadly Orgone Radiation (or DOR) and goes into battle against it...

He even tries to explain Freud's Death Instinct (without the instinct) as a perception of DOR.

But it is no longer merely Eros and Thanatos battling for the human soul. It's a Cosmic Space War between OR and DOR....

In March 1952 the DOR clouds hover over Orgonon. They come in from the west and cause a 'stillness' and 'bleakness' over the area. All sounds of life disappear. The birds stop singing. The frogs stop croaking, the birds hide in the trees. Leaves drop from branches.

If Orgone energy is the motor force of Orgasm = Health, then DOR must be the destructive energy which represses sexuality = Disease. But WR reckons DOR is not as powerful as OR and can eventually be swept out of the Universe. That's why he invents the CLOUD-BUSTER...

THE CLOUDBUSTER?

Sure. This is a group of hollow pipes on a turntable which can be turned and pointed in any direction.

The pipes are connected to cables placed in a source of flowing water.

These pipes are supposed to draw the DOR out of the clouds.

The water in turn draws the DOR out of the pipes and neutralises it.

Imagine a lightning rod for orgone rather than electricity, and you're getting close to the idea.

DRAW

CLOUDBUSTER

DRAW WATER

DRAW

...WHAT ELSE CAN THE CLOUDBUSTER DO?

It can create or
break up cloud
formations when
the pipes are
pointed in one
direction for a
long time, thereby
creating concentra-
tions of orgone
energy.

In effect, it de-
pollutes or cleans
up the air. The
whole process is
called Cosmic
Orgone Radiation
Engineering (CORE).

But if the Earth has become a 'desert', and if the
Cloudbuster is the divining rod of the heavens,
surely it can make rain as well...

In 1954, Reich goes out to Arizona for OROP desert
(Orgone Energy Operation in the desert)

There's absolutely
no reason for rain
to fall there, but...

PHOENIX GAZETTE

STRANGE RAINFALL

Tucson Post

HEAVENS OPEN

ARIZONA STAR

SCIENTIST MAKES RAIN
WITH 'CLOUDBUSTER'

OXENICXST

Quo Vadis, WR?

If concentrations
of OR can clear the
air of DOR and
fructify the deserts,
what else can it do
in these American
1950's?

Well, it can
(AND SHOULD)
be used to combat
the growing menace
of ATOMIC ENERGY.

The US Government
has already dropped
its T N T eggs on
Hiroshima and
Nagasaki, developed
a Hydrogen Bomb
and is testing its
new toys —where?
in the American
Desert...

But Nuclear Energy
doesn't quite fit into
the Orgone cosmology.

Reich allows it to
become the one
energy source out-
side the system and
therefore at war with
OR in the struggle
for the Universe

DOR = Nuclear Energy

...IT'S TIME FOR THE ORANUR EXPERIMENT

With ORANUR, Reich hopes to heal radiation poisoning with orgone, by use of the Accumulator, leading to nothing less than... IMMUNIZATION of All mankind against nuclear fallout!

But...

...RADIATION POISONING. WE'D BETTER STOP ORANUR

But not before he concludes that, what we have so far thought of as radiation sickness caused by the effect of nuclear radiation on human tissue IS NOT THAT AT ALL. What is it then?

A SEVERE REACTION OF THE ORGANISMIC OR ENERGY AGAINST THE ACTION OF NUCLEAR ENERGY (NR) RADIATION.

It would seem that the terrible disaster of the Oranur Experiment would somehow narrow the illimitable horizons of our Hero. It doesn't. After all, the heavy concentrations of DOR in the atmosphere have to find some explanation, especially in a universe so obsessed with Friends and Enemies.

Reich now becomes convinced that UFOs (or Ea's as he calls them) are fuelled by Orgone and that DOR is the EXHAUST OF THESE MACHINES.

The Earth is under attack from outer space and spaceships have landed near Orgonon.

If he can find a way to use the Cloud-buster as a space-gun, he can make contact with them.

Who are the GOOD GUYS in this movie?

THE US AIR FORCE IS PROTECTING ME.

EISENHOWER KNOWS THE VALUE OF MY WORK, BUT HE'S NOT AT LIBERTY TO ADMIT IT

WHY NOT?

HE'S PROBABLY PREVENTED FROM DOING SO BY THE **HIGs**.

THE HIGS?

HIGs = Hoodlums In Government.

There will also later be the CORE-Men (Cosmic Orgone Radiation Engineers) from outer space who will come to fight DOR and the Emotional Plague. Reich will claim that one of these is his father who had mated with his earthly mother.

161

So, to RECAP:

WR, aka SO, upon discovering OR, enters battle against EP, only to find the 'Ea's are threatening the Le with DOR in collusion with the HIGs and waits for the COREs to save the day!

Re-enter the FDA

In Reich's own private vocabulary they've been lurking in the 'bushes' while he himself is on the 'meadow'

Call it what you will, they've come to bust him...

In 1954 they bring an injunction against him, on the basis of having sold the Accumulators across state lines.

WR thinks himself above the courts and fails to appear.

TO APPEAR IN COURT AS A 'DEFENDANT' WOULD REQUIRE DISCLOSURE OF EVIDENCE IN SUPPORT OF THE POSITION OF THE DISCOVERY OF THE LIFE ENERGY. SUCH DISCLOSURE, HOWEVER, WOULD INVOKE UNTOLD COMPLICATIONS, AND POSSIBLY, **NATIONAL DISASTER**.

IN ANY CASE, SCIENTIFIC MATTERS CANNOT POSSIBLY BE DECIDED UPON IN COURT.

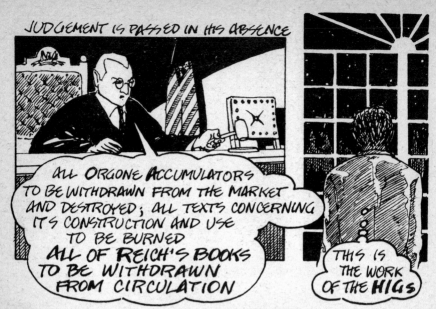

Reich fails to comply with the court order and, in 1955, an action of criminal contempt is filed against him. This time he chooses to fight the case with himself as lawyer or Counsel for the Discovery of Life Energy...

164

YOU LEFT A BIT ON THAT ONE

LET'S THROW THESE IN FOR GOOD MEASURE

And on August 23, 1956, twenty-three years after the Nazi book bonfires, the US Govt puts a second match to Reich's words.

At the Gansevoort Incinerator in New York all materials dealing with the Accumulator are burned.

Also burned are: THE MURDER OF CHRIST, PEOPLE IN TROUBLE, COSMIC SUPERIMPOSITION, ETHER, GOD AND DEVIL, none of which mentions the Accumulator...

WR in Prison, sees himself as a martyr successor to Socrates, Christ, Bruno, Ghandi, Luther.
He waits for his 'Protectors', top officials on the US Government, to get him out. Failing that, the CORE-men will have to spring him.

He works in the prison library in Lewisburg, Penn.

On November 3
1957
while still a
prisoner,
WR'S heart
attacks him
and
he is buried
in the
mausoleum
he built
specially
to perpetuate
his image
at
ORGONON.

In the 1960's some
street libertarians
will try to claim WR
as a champion for
what they call their
Sexual Revolution.

NOT THIS
'FUCKER CHAOS',
NOT ME,
THAT'S NOT ME.

He had even
begun calling
sexual intercourse
THE GENITAL
EMBRACE

Otherwise,
the established worlds
of
left-wing politics,
psychoanalysis
and science,
try to write him off
as a LUNATIC.

Love
IS
PEACE

Let's see what's gone on in the world since the LUNATIC left it...

The left-wing parties, free from the pressure of the PERSONAL, dry up and become more and more remote from people's daily lives, some even promote nuclear power.

Well-fed psychoanalysts turn 'cured' neurotics out into 'normal' streets

We've got rid of that dangerous Orgone Accumulator, but psychiatry still has electroshock-therapy and chemical suppressants in its arsenal.

WR's radical theories of child-rearing are consigned to the dustbin while closet authoritarians and sex-role enforcers, most notably Dr Spock, become best sellers.

WHOA!

BEFORE YOU CAN BE TRUSTED WITH A POWERFUL BODY AND FULL-GROWN INSTINCTS, YOU MUST FIRST LEARN TO CONTROL YOUR WISHES AND INSTINCTS FOR THE SAKE OF OTHERS AND UNDERSTAND THE LAWS OF CONDUCT IN THE WORLD OUTSIDE YOUR FAMILY

Let's hear what the father of the 'permissive society' has to say in 1970...

NO DATING UNTIL SIXTEEN.

NO PETTING UNTIL YOU ARE 'GOING STEADY' FOR AT LEAST A YEAR, NO KISSING FOR ANOTHER YEAR AND ONLY AFTER COMMITMENT TO MARRIAGE, ...OF COURSE NO SEX BEFORE MARRIAGE

Meanwhile, somewhere in space...

Back on Earth life just carries on as usual, free of EP and DOR.

And last, but not LEAST: the SANE SCIENTISTS...

The End!

THIS REALLY IS A CONSPIRACY

While WR, one of a long line of Great HEALERS and Medicine Men, who played out his own image in the Heavens and insisted his METAPHOR was FACT, floats perhaps on a Cosmic Orgone Ocean or is just plain old OR... (Organically Rotting)

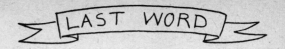

WR is currently 'enjoying' a revival as he did in the 1960's, in no small way due to the first really important Reich biography, **Fury on Earth** by Myron Sharaf. It is best to begin reading Reich with an overview like Sharaf's; otherwise, it is impossible to know where to start. Once in America Reich revised much of his early work to conform to the principles of orgonomy. What we read now, especially in English, of the classics — **Function of the Orgasm, The Sexual Revolution, Mass Psychology of Fascism** — are not the original works. Reich's own political autobiography, **People in Trouble**, although containing sections written in the 1930's and 1940's, was added to, updated and only published in 1953. The American edition of **The Mass Psychology of Fascism** neatly exorcises such anti-Americanisms (WR himself now anti-Red) as 'Communist', 'Socialist', 'class consciousness', etc. It is important to remember that Reich's current trustees, editors, translators, etc. are chiefly Americans who knew him only towards the end of his life, in his American phase, and who generally share in his 'anti-political' bias. Reading Reich is a road full of deep pits. Without the complete landscape you never know how far you've come.

One day you might tumble (literally) into the hands of a 'Reichian', 'neo-Reichian' or 'post-Reichian' therapist. If so, keep in mind that there are numerous interpretations of their respective roles in the general 'Reichian' picture, and that their work, at most, evolves only from a small part of

Reich's. They reflect WR's more 'private' phase. These are not the inheriting sons of the man who arranged illegal abortions in healthy conditions, who drove around Vienna handing out free contraceptives to teenagers, who fought to affirm and not merely tolerate childhood sexuality, or even the 'madman' who said: 'We shall have to learn to counteract the murderous form of atomic energy with the life-furthering function of orgone energy and thus render it harmless.'

VDT=DOR?

The video display terminals (VDT) widely used by authors and publishers and preferred to the outmoded typewriter have been the subject of medical studies as well as restrictive legislation in recent months. Many people who use these electronic wonders have been found to suffer from eyestrain and fatigue, backaches, headaches, psychological stress as well as carpal tunnel syndrome, an inflammation of wrist ligaments that ultimately can cause a person to lose strength in his or her grip. The most significant studies concern the dangerous levels of radiation emitted by VDTs and the harmful effects of these on pregnant women.

The original manuscript of this book was typed on an Imperial manual typewriter made in Leicester, England circa 1945.